TreeHouses

Living a Dream

TreeHouses
Living a Dream

HARPER
DESIGN

An Imprint of HarperCollins*Publishers*

TREEHOUSES: LIVING A DREAM
Copyright © 2005 by HARPER DESIGN and LOFT Publications

First published in 2005 by:
Harper Design
An Imprint of HarperCollins*Publishers*
10 East 53rd Street
New York, NY 10022
Tel.: (212) 207-7000
Fax: (212) 207-7654
HarperDesign@harpercollins.com
www.harpercollins.com

Distributed throughout the world by:
HarperCollins International
10 East 53rd Street
New York, NY 10022
Fax: (212) 207-7654

HarperCollins books may be purchased for educational, business, or sales promotional use.
For information, please write: Special Markets Department, HarperCollins Publishers Inc.,
10 East 53rd Street, New York, NY 10022

Publisher:
Paco Asensio

Editorial Coordination:
Alejandro Bahamón

Translation:
Ana G. Cañizares

Art Director:
Mireia Casanovas Soley

Graphic Design and Layout:
Emma Termes Parera

Library of Congress Cataloging-in-Publication Data

Bahamón, Alejandro.
  Treehouses: Living a Dream / by Alejandro Bahamón.
      p. cm.
  ISBN 0-06-078001-0 (hardcover)
  1. Tree houses. I. Title: Tree houses: living a dream. II. Title.
  TH4885.B34 2005
  728'.9--dc22
                        2004029898

Printed by:
Cayfosa-Quebecor. Spain

D.L:B-9.289-2005

First Printing, 2005

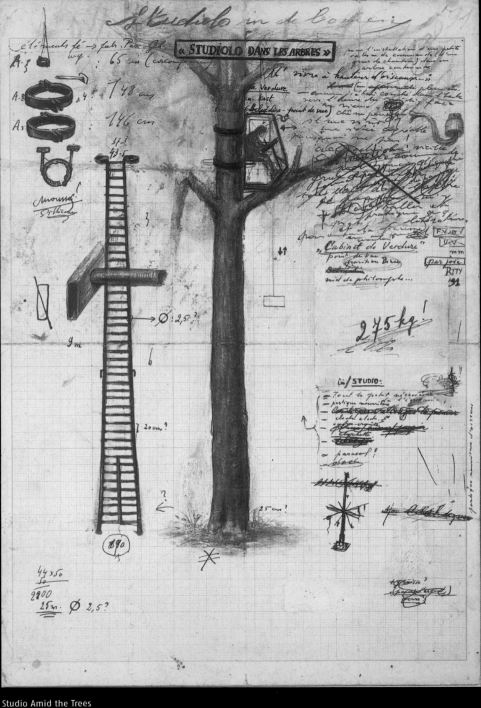

Studio Amid the Trees
Artist: Thierry de Cordier

It seems that the idea of building a small refuge amid the trees is a concept that man has entertained since the beginning of his existence. In spite of this, only a limited amount of graphical documentation exists to illustrate its origins and trace its evolution throughout history, probably due to the ephemeral quality of these constructions. In any case, it is evident that tree houses are not a contemporary invention. In certain cultures of the South Pacific, entire populations once lived among the trees to protect themselves from the dangers of being at ground level and to obtain better watch posts. Records also document observation bridges in Japan, luxurious platforms in Persia and classical Rome, and a popularized version of the tree house during Britain's Victorian era. Although in the majority of cases this type of construction has been generated in a spontaneous manner, much like vernacular architecture, it is an exercise in design that continues to attract a multitude of architects and designers to its unique characteristics.

One of the main determinants in the design of any architectural project is the site in which it is located and, consequently, the relationship intended between the object and its surroundings. Factors such as location, inclination, accessibility, light, ventilation, views, and many more considerations directly influence the general composition, form, construction, and structure of the project. Hardly any other type of project, however, could have such a close relationship with its surroundings as a tree house. From the election of the site to the construction details, its design is closely tied to the characteristics of the tree chosen to harbor the house. These structures rest on living foundations that are at times fragile, difficult to access, and in continuous movement caused by their growth or the effects of the wind. As such, a tree house's existence greatly depends on the resistance and vitality of the tree, a factor that has generated a variety of tree houses as rich as that of the trees that exist on the planet.

The following pages illustrate a detailed and varied selection of the most recently built tree houses around the world—from lookout towers in Tasmania, for the protection of forests that are home to the largest hardwood trees in the world, to the latest works by TreeHouse Company, considered one of the leading firms of the construction of tree houses in the UK. The diversity of their functions range from a suspended sauna on a small Finnish island to a cabin designated to shelter protesters against deforestation in Seville, in the south of Spain. Despite the variety of their geographical positions and the numerous variables that envelop them, however, tree houses can be grouped into a set of clearly defined typologies according to how they are inserted into a particular tree. These typologies, into which the projects of this book have been divided, are represented by small pictograms (see pages 8 and 9) that identify each type of tree house and its tree placement design. As this book illustrates, these tree house concepts can be translated into diverse architectural projects, anything from the use of hand-crafted organic materials to computer-generated models produced by the most advanced computer programs.

AROUND THE TRUNK

This type of tree house is often very stable, given that it takes advantage of the sturdiness of tree trunks with large diameters, and normally occupies the lower or middle section of the tree. Conifers like the pine or the cypress—or other more mature trees that offer an exceptionally solid base, such as the oak or poplar—are ideal for these kinds of constructions. The trunk plays a crucial role in these cabins not only because it acts as the main structural pillar, but also because the general composition of the project revolves around it.

SUPPORTED BY SEVERAL TREES

This scheme offers great flexibility in terms of the placement, form, and size of the tree house. The distribution of weight and tension among various points can enable the creation of separate complexes right in the middle of the forest. Nevertheless, the design should ensure a flexible structure to prevent the swaying of each tree from damaging the tree house. Generally, this can be achieved by joining the different platforms with suspended bridges, or by fastening supportive beams with flexible latches that permit the trunks to move freely.

SUSPENDED FROM SEVERAL TREES

Few examples of this type of tree house exist today, although it is one of the most attractive models due to the unique sensation generated by a floating structure. The most relevant problems associated with this type of structure involve assembling and dismantling difficulties, as well as the accessibility of the cabin once assembled. Out of all types of tree houses, this model is surely the one to offer the best panoramic views of its surroundings, which is why it is common to find examples of lookout towers designed according to this system.

ON TOP OF BRANCHES

The branches of a tree, which normally extend horizontally and in some cases toward the ground, are ideal for installing platforms of this sort. Trees that adhere to this type of composition, such as beech, cedar, apple, and variations of the pine or plane tree, are the favorites of children for climbing. The need to find the most appropriate spot that requires the least amount of additional supports for the tree house can lead to its placement anywhere on the tree.

ON THE REMAINS OF A TREE

As a result of natural ageing processes, natural occurrences like lightning bolts, or the intervention of man, many architects are faced with the challenge of inactive trees. Even though a tree may be completely inert, the dimensions of the trunk and its firm attachment to the ground render it an ideal site on which to build a tree house. Large, solid trees are the most appropriate for this purpose, assuring a stable support for the new structure and its long duration under adequate maintenance.

ALONGSIDE A TREE

Some tree houses do not incorporate the tree itself as a support mechanism, yet integrate themselves into the wooded landscape so exceptionally that they can well be considered tree houses in their own right. This integration can be achieved in various ways: by a structure that revolves around a tree, an elevated platform above a dense forest, or a construction that adapts to the structure and composition of the tree in question.

Island Wood Bog

Architect: Mithun Architects

Location: Bainbridge Island, WA, USA

Photos: Art Grice Photography

Structural system:

Steel rings and stainless steel locks that adapt to the growth of the tree

Materials:

Recycled fir tree wood for the structure and cedar strips, folding doors salvaged from an old boat, and copper sheets for the ventilation slots

Type of tree:

Douglas fir

This tree house forms part of an educational complex located in the south of Bainbridge Island in Washington State, USA. The complex is responsible for the restoration of swamps, streams, and ponds, as well as the natural habitat of salmon, currently in danger of extinction. The school offers young students a thorough knowledge of the natural environment through manual projects and outdoor studies. Fourth- and fifth-grade students designate certain days to the exploration of the natural characteristics of the area. In designing the cabin, the architects chose to observe how the natural inhabitants of trees construct their homes, rather than relying on the archetypal tree house that we are most familiar with—creating an object inspired by the forms of beehives and cocoons. The result is an evocative and unconventional learning space for groups of children, professors, and environmental guides. The heavily inclined walls and roof grant an extensively high ceiling that generates a strong connection with the vertical mass of the tree.

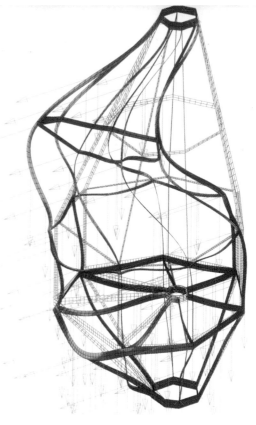

Structure scheme

The cabins, located adjacent to a natural swamp, offer a refuge from continuous showers, as well as the opportunity to enjoy magnificent panoramic views of the area. The company Tree House Workshop collaborated in the design and construction of the project.

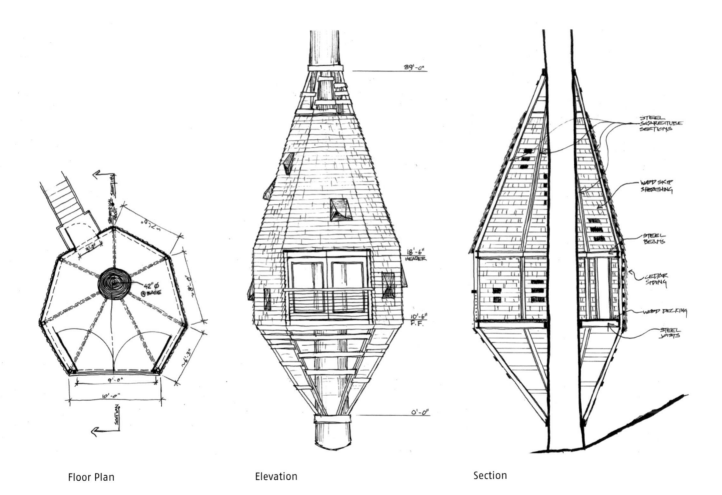

Floor Plan   Elevation   Section

The concentric composition around the tree trunk affords this tree house great stability.
The floor plan consists of a symmetrical form with seven sides, the largest of which
was chosen for the installation of the window.

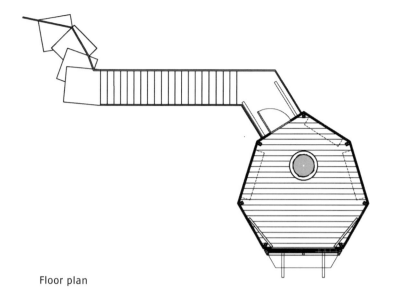

Floor plan

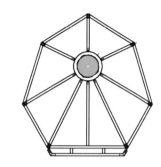

Structure plan

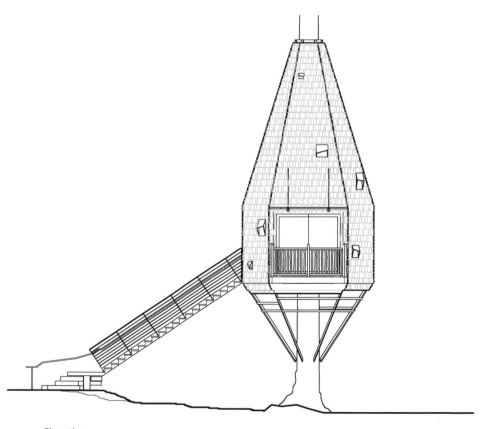

Elevation

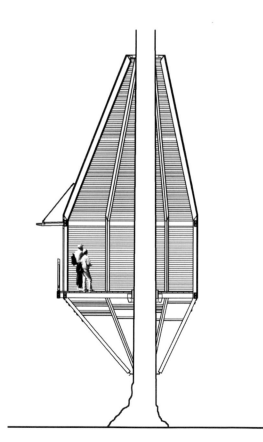

Section

Tree Tectonics

Architect: Urban Studio
Location: Atlanta, GA, USA
Photos: Urban Studio

Structural system:

Cedar pillars and taut steel wires

Materials:

Cedar and oak

Type of tree:

Oak

Tree Tectonics is a project that formed part of an exhibition on tree houses at Atlanta's Botanic Garden in June 2003. Urban Studio was the winner of the design contest, in which the participants could choose one of the 11 locations designated to these small projects as the future site for its construction. The contest's criteria clearly prohibited nailing directly into the tree or damaging it in any way. Other factors taken into account in choosing the winning project included its accessibility, the creative use of materials, its durability, and its interaction with nature. After being selected for construction, this tree house was built in two months, the first of which was employed to prefabricate the different components inside a warehouse and the second to transport them and assemble them on-site.

This project aims to explore the diverse relations between architecture and nature through the study of movement, structure, and form in the layout of the project, as well as in its three-dimensional elements.

The structural approach—derived from the tree itself, which serves
as the main support for the elevated platform—expresses its balance
with nature through its streamlined geometry and architectural elements.

Inspired by the form of a snail shell and the existing spiral staircase,
the architects created a platform that revolves around the tree.

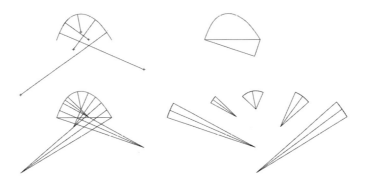

Preliminary diagrams

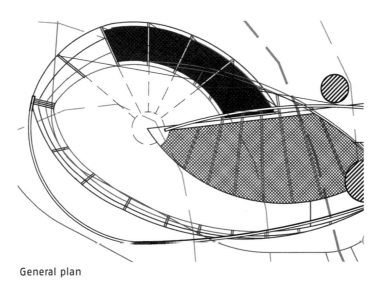

General plan

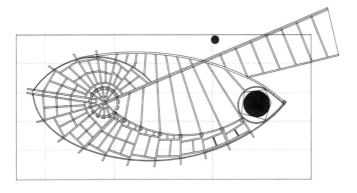

Structure plan

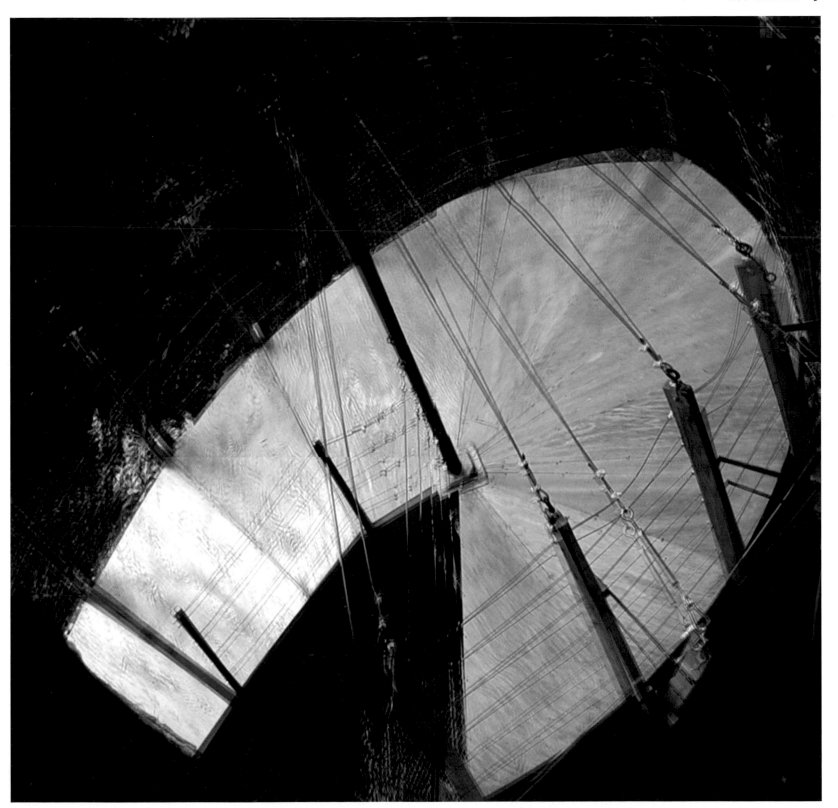

Insect House

Architect: Santiago Cirgueda
Location: Seville, Spain
Photos: Santiago Cirgueda

Structural system:

Steel rings and cantilevers

Materials:

Steel cladding, curved metal sheets, and PVC foam

Type of tree:

Poplar, pine, and plane

The Insect House arose as an idea of protest against the deforestation of La Alameda in the center of Seville, Spain. According to the architect, the project goes further than simply making an ecological statement on the protection of endangered trees; it proposes a strategy of opposition toward the eviction and relocation of the local population and the deterioration of their current lifestyle. Following the fundamental premises of an efficient urban guerrilla, a series of modules were designed to adhere to the trees with parts that can be assembled on-site. A 40-foot platform, a lower shell that acts as storage, and a protective sliding upper shell form a body that incorporates an unusual ventilation system that runs continually through the interior to generate a pleasant temperature during the summer months. The shells give shelter to one person and offer protection from the elements.

The assembly strategy for this tree house requires four people
during a maximum estimated time of two hours.

Assembly process

The assembly process of the project is composed of three stages that involve anchoring the main support around the tree, applying the metallic skeleton of the cabin, and, finally, installing the enveloping structure.

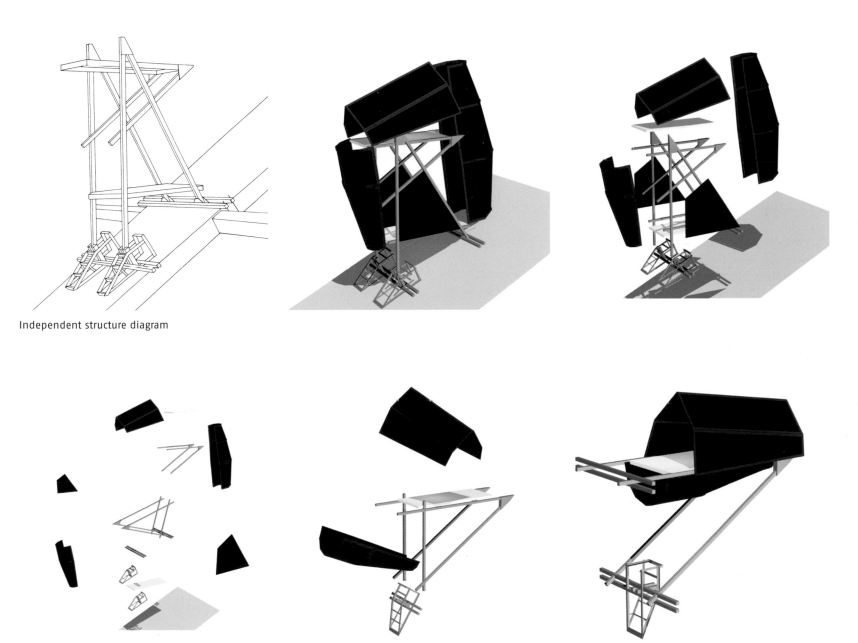

Independent structure diagram

Tree structure diagram

Robinson

Architect: TreeHouse Company
Location: Hampshire, UK
Photos: TreeHouse Company

Structural system:

Radial portico system formed by a central ring around the trunk and eight support points along the circumference

Materials:

Douglas fir for the structure, supportive elements, and exterior finishes; cedar panels for the roof; Willow panels for the handrail

Type of tree:

Old English oak

This pavilion was constructed in the backyard of a vacation home in Hampshire, UK. The family wanted to have a playground area for the children that could also be used as a guest room, dining area, or relaxing refuge in the garden from which to enjoy the landscape without having to worry about the existing climatic conditions. The presence of a large, mature oak tree was taken advantage of as the main structural and composition element of the project. The tree house was constructed around a central ring that embraces the trunk and a series of auxiliary supports that create a radial scheme, allowing optimal views of the entire garden. A broad spiral staircase leads to the large, main platform, which is covered by a cedar-paneled ceiling and divided into an open and a closed area. A steeper staircase can be accessed from here to reach an outdoor platform that serves as a lookout point.

The first platform is accessed by a wide staircase to accommodate
not only children, but also adults, for family get-togethers.

The second platform, situated on a higher level, takes advantage of the tree's branches, which invite visitors to climb its ladder-like structure.

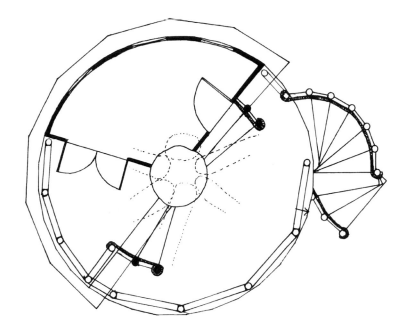

Floor plan

Elevation

Attached Tree House

Architect: Softroom
Location: Virtual
Photos: Softroom

Structural system:

Light frames and platforms
supported by metal rings

Materials:

Metal rings, frames, and cables;
plastic and elastic membranes

Type of tree:

Any type of tree

This is one of four projects conceived by this group of architects for *Wallpaper* magazine. The only condition posed by the design was that of creating a tree house. The resulting concept was to create a very light structure that could be easily transported and attached to a tree while causing minimal impact. The structure combines a variety of "living" components that include a picnic table, a bed, and numerous observation platforms. Although the project is a study on the form, structure, and function of a tree house whose prototype has never been built, its structural system is a plausible one from which real models can be generated. The project not only proposes a simple and quick assembly, but also an entire system of cables that can be extended to neighboring trees and thus create a network throughout the surrounding forest. Solar panels, gas containers, and water channeled from the nearest source achieve a sustainable structure that carries out all of the basic functions of a home.

High-tech computer drawing programs were used for the design of this project,
which allowed not only the visualization of the general composition from any angle,
but also the appearance of textures and materials for a truly realistic effect.

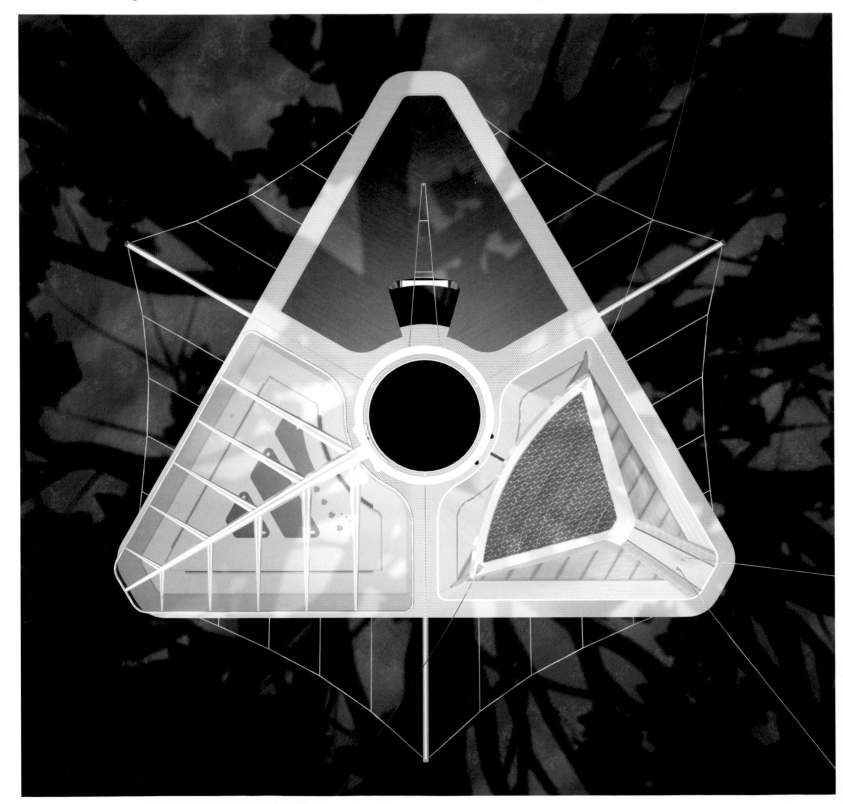

The first ring serves as a support for the light frame that sustains the living and service areas.
A second ring, on the upper level, supports the structure upon which the roof rests.

Plendelhof

Architect: Andreas Wenning / baumraum
Location: Plendelhof, Germany
Photos: Alasdair Jardine

Structural system:

Rings and steel cables

Materials:

Steel for the supporting
elements and wood

Type of tree:

Beech

This tree house was built between two beech trees in Plendelhof, about 20 miles south of Bremen, Germany. The clients, owners of an equestrian ranch, wanted to have a small structure within the trees in order to take advantage of the private landscape, and to observe the treetops and distant views. The goal was to create a comfortable space with a minimum surface area for relaxing and occasionally sleeping, incorporating a south-facing balcony for sunbathing. Before proceeding with the design, the architects searched for the most appropriate tree for the construction of the tree house, which in this case turned out to be a pair of beech trees chosen for their firm trunks and strong branches. Provisional platforms were then laid out to determine the ideal height for the tree house and the points from which to suspend the structure. After much study, it was decided that in order to avoid damage to the trees as much as possible, prefabricated elements constructed prior to their assembly would constitute the main bulk of the project. This system would also make it possible to dismantle the tree house during bad-weather seasons, thus preventing its deterioration.

The main platform's triangular form and the structural system of taut cables are reminiscent of a boat structure.

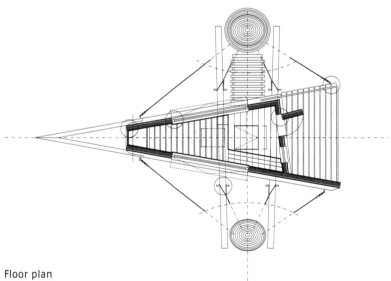

Floor plan

A second, less inclined staircase, supported by the first,
allows for safer and easier access to the interior.

Swift

Architect: TreeHouse Company
Location: Mid Wales, UK
Photos: Redcover / Chris Tubbs

Structural system:

Wooden cantilevers attached to the trees and additional wooden pillars in the ground

Materials:

Red pine for the structure and general finishings; felt lining along the ceiling; rope and softwood for the balcony

Type of tree:

Beech and ash

This tree house is the product of a contest held by the TreeHouse Company in which 600 children participated in designing their ideal treehouse. The winning project belonged to six children from three different families, and for whom the TreeHouse Company built the tree house free of charge. The project consists of a lookout platform suspended from a mature beech tree located on the high side of a narrow wooded valley in Mid Wales, UK. A rope bridge hangs from the central platform and leads to a smaller platform surrounded by ash trees that alludes to the form of a ship, given its bow shape, portholes, and anchor. The use of rope as an element of security and to define spaces accentuates this analogy. The tree house is used by children and adults as a rest area from which to explore the forest and enjoy views of the surrounding valley.

A remarkably warm and comfortable space was created
with the simple use of a few rustic furnishings made of natural fibers,
such as the rug, various cushions, and wicker baskets.

The only alteration with respect to the original version designed by the children was the access stairway, which would have incorporated an old trunk that was considered too dangerous to maintain.

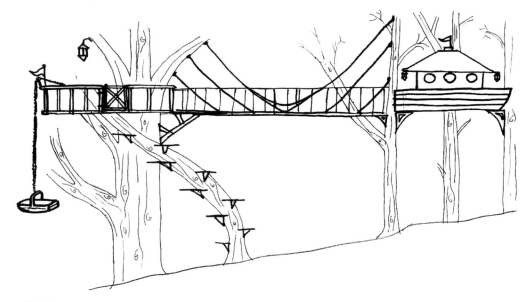

Sketch

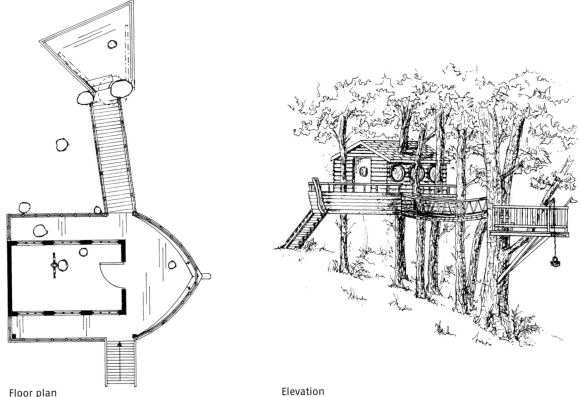

Floor plan

Elevation

Mathews

Architect: TreeHouse Company
Location: Oxford, UK
Photos: TreeHouse Company

Structural system:

Wooden cantilevers

Materials:

Douglas fir cladding, cedar
planks, and willow wood panels

Type of tree:

Horse chestnut and oak

This tree house is a small complex comprised of interior and exterior platforms that provide a dynamic playground for children and adolescents. The structure is supported by a horse chestnut tree and two oak trees inside a yard in Oxford, UK, and is composed of various platforms interconnected by suspended bridges, rope ladders, and rope nets. The design was based on the organic forms of the trees themselves, generating a series of sloping and undulating roofs and handmade windows. Two enclosed spaces can be used for parties or to sleep over in, while other exterior platforms can be used for play or rest. The exterior cladding is finished in Douglas fir and the ceilings are fabricated with cedar planks.

The brackets that sustain the main platforms are also supported by complementary poles anchored to the ground.

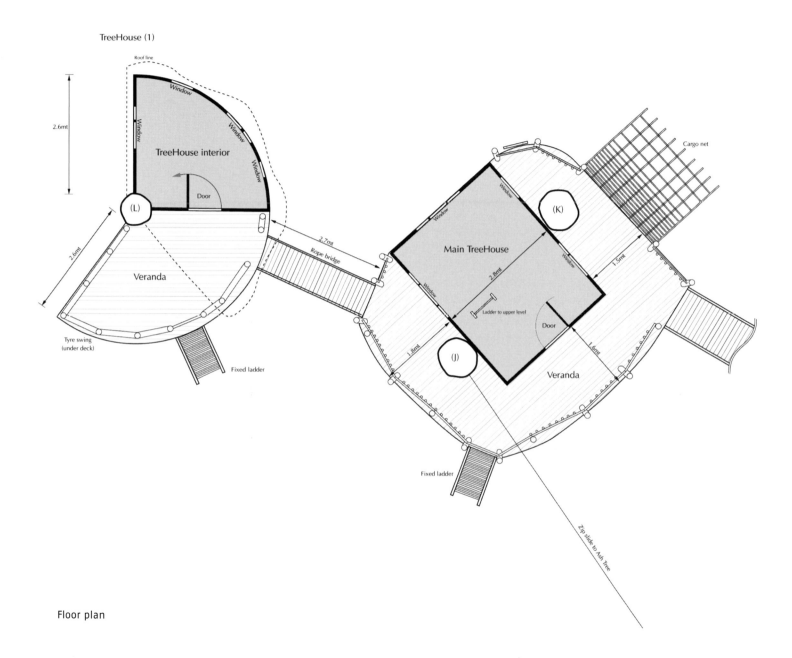

TreeHouse (1)

Roof line

2.6mt

Window

Window

TreeHouse interior

Window

Window

(L)

Door

2.6mt

Veranda

2.7mt

Rope bridge

Cargo net

Window

Window

(K)

Main TreeHouse

2.8mt

1.5mt

Window

Ladder to upper level

Door

1.8mt

(J)

1.6mt

Veranda

Tyre swing
(under deck)

Fixed ladder

Fixed ladder

Zip slide to Ash Tree

Floor plan

The organization of the two structures uses organic forms for the exterior platforms
that are contrasted with the geometric and linear design of the interior spaces.

Wencke

Architect: Andreas Wenning / baumraum
Location: Bremerhaven, Germany
Photos: Alasdair Jardine

Structural system:

Wooden beams supported by metal cables

Materials:

Metal for the cables and anchors; wood for the general structure

Type of tree:

Ash and elm

The Wenke family, for whom this tree house was built, yearned for a place within their densely wooded garden in which adults and children alike could pass the time and either play, relax, or stay over as guests. The west side of the property harbored two rows of trees and a small structure in which to make fires that seemed like the ideal location for the tree house. Two ash trees and adjacent elm trees with 15- to 20-inch diameters were chosen to accommodate the structure. The project was designed to make the best use of the surrounding conditions, as well as to satisfy the clients' needs. The result is a tree house with a spacious interior that can entertain the entire family during leisure time or sleep two adults on large mattresses. The exterior platform extends toward the fireplace and the windows allow framed views of the surrounding landscape.

The geometric composition of this project was achieved through various openings
within the volume, which permit the contemplation of the landscape from diverse perspectives,
and the dynamic spatial layout of the interior of the tree house.

The design process involved the creation of full-scale models that were installed within the trees in order to carefully analyze the best conditions for the final project.

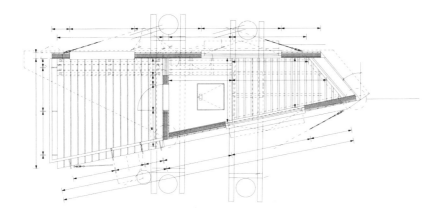

Floor plan

Elevations

General section

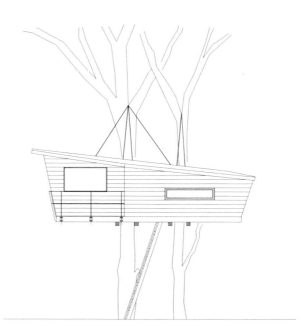

General elevation

De Hann

Architect: TreeHouse Company
Location: Kent, UK
Photos: TreeHouse Company

Structural system:

The distribution is open so that each area remains free of any strictly defined borders.

Materials:

Douglas fir, bamboo sticks, South African cane, English heather, Scandinavian redwood, and rope

Type of tree:

Chestnut

The clients of this tree house, an adult couple frequently visited by their grandchildren, wanted to take advantage of the rear part of the yard that includes a small lake. The tree house was designated as a small space in which to sit and relax while contemplating the landscape. The project consists of a main cabin linked to two suspended platforms by way of hanging rope bridges. The structure can be accessed three different ways: by a broad spiral staircase more appropriate for adults, or by two vertical ladders made of bamboo sticks that offer a more playful venue for the children. Fir tree wood was used for the general structure because of its resistance and flexibility, while the English heather was used for the interior finishings, the South African cane for the ceiling, the redwood for the balconies, and the bamboo sticks for the handrails and staircases.

The main characteristic of this tree house is the dominant presence of bamboo sticks, used to construct the beams, columns, roof, and handrails.

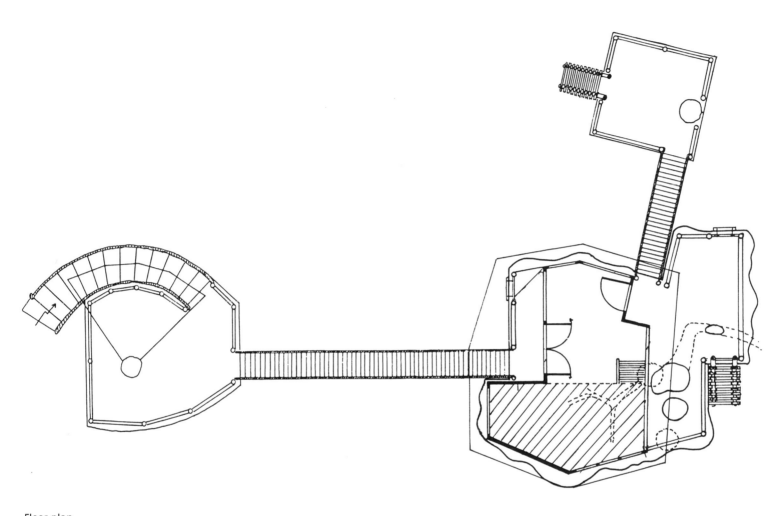

Floor plan

The tree house is also used by the children to camp in or sleep in overnight.

Girls' Tree Houses

Architect: Alain Laurens
Location: Provence, France
Photos: Pere Planells

Structural system:

Brackets supported by the trunk and complementary wood pillars anchored directly into the ground

Materials:

Pine, profiled metal cladding, taut steel cable, and rope

Type of tree:

Oak

This tree house, made up of two small rooms and a series of platforms and suspended bridges, was created as a rest area and playground for the client's two daughters. The sturdiness of the trees inside this yard in Provence, in the south of France, offered the ideal conditions to create a secure structure that comes close to that of a conventional ground-level construction. The inclination of the terrain permits access to the tree house by way of a suspended bridge fastened to either tree by two steel cables, which in turn define the handrail made from rope. The interior of the tree houses, equipped with folding glass windows and numerous furnishings, is prepared to receive guests for play, study, or sleep. A series of exterior walkways connect the two tree houses, as well as various stairways that access the ground and blend in with the existing plants.

The interior furnishings were fabricated to meet the daily needs of the little girls for whom this tree house was created, transforming it into a space adequately prepared for frequent and permanent use.

The final touch to the composition is a small wooden deck that enjoys
broad panoramic views of the narrow valley that surrounds the tree houses.

Two Tree Houses

Architect: Jeff Etelamaki
Location: Princeton, NJ, USA
Photos: Jeff Etelamaki

Structural system:

Steel rings and wooden beams

Materials:

Cedar

Type of tree:

Pine

The design of this project was initially inspired by the drawings of two boys, aged seven and nine, who would eventually become the occupants of the tree house. Each boy desired his own independent cabin that would connect with the other by way of a bridge and other playful means that would allow the boys to entertain themselves. In fulfillment of their wish, the design and structural planning of the project had to respond not only to the fluctuating growth patterns of each tree, but also to the activity that occurs between them. Each piece rests on an independent structure, employing flexible connections between them that avoid possible damage due to high winds or the future growth of the trees themselves. The formal result of each tree house responds to the different natural structures of each individual tree. While one of the parts is supported by a rubber component that embraces the longitudinal trunk of the tree, the other is supported along various points that allow numerous branches to pierce through the floor, walls, and roof panels.

From a distance, the tree house complex initially appears as a suspended, sealed box amid the trees; but a closer look reveals the image of a composition of open and closed surfaces that interact with the exterior.

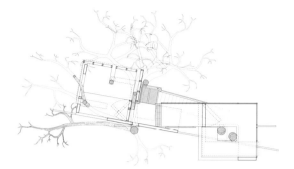

Floor plan

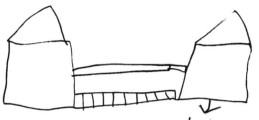

Leak proof roof
at least 1 window
a door that
closes.
a rug

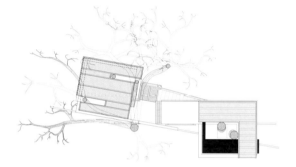

Roof plan

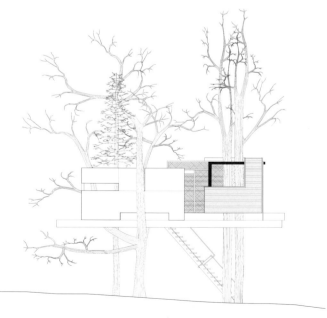

Elevation

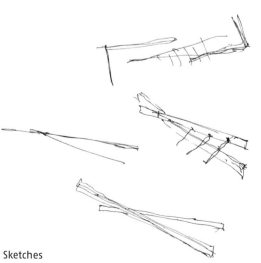

Sketches

A great variety of inexpensive and lightweight materials
were chosen for the construction of both tree houses,
generating a unique and original project that adapts to the environment.

Rescue Station

Architect: Andrew Maynard

Location: Styx Valley, Tasmania, Australia

Photos: Andrew Maynard

Structural system:

Metal rings, extendable tubes, and metal frames

Materials:

Metal for the structure and wood for the paneling and interior finishings

Type of tree:

Hardwood

The Styx Valley is a dense forest in the south of Tasmania, home to the largest hardwood trees in the world. They can easily reach 260 feet in height and over 400 years in age. It is one of the earth's most unique and richest ecosystems, yet a fragile one nonetheless. A large surface area of this forest forms part of the Southwest National Park and is protected as a nature reserve. However, a considerable part of this forest finds itself outside of these borders and under the indiscriminate exploitation of lumber businesses. In an effort to protect this area, a great number of activists have protested and formed human barricades to halt the razing. The objective of this small pavilion is to support this cause by serving as a rescue and surveillance station. The project consists of a suspended tree house supported by three trees, not only protecting these trees, but also providing ample surveillance views around each lookout tower. The presence of several such towers would be enough to cover a vast region of the park.

Each tree house is made up of two levels. The lower floor provides space
for the investigation and service areas, while the upper floor houses a rest
and sleeping area for up to three persons.

Lifepod Project

Architect: Kyu Che Studio
Location: Virtual
Photos: Kyu Che

Structural system:

Taut steel cables and rings

Materials:

Plywood, cables, and extend-able stainless steel tubes

Type of tree:

Coniferous and large trees

The Lifepod consists of a small oval-shaped cabin that can be easily transported and assembled in diverse natural settings. The pod can be set up directly on-site and used as a small office or guest room in the backyard, or hidden well inside a densely wooded forest. A system of extendable steel legs enables the pod to rise several yards aboveground, while another mechanism comprised of stainless steel cables permits the structure to be suspended at a greater height. The cables are anchored to large trees by metal braces coated in rubber to protect the trunk. Despite its reduced proportions, the oval shape of the cabin generates an effect of spaciousness inside, fully equipped with the necessary services to accommodate two people for several days. Two sides of the tree house are defined by sliding glass doors that allow for a complete integration with the surrounding landscape.

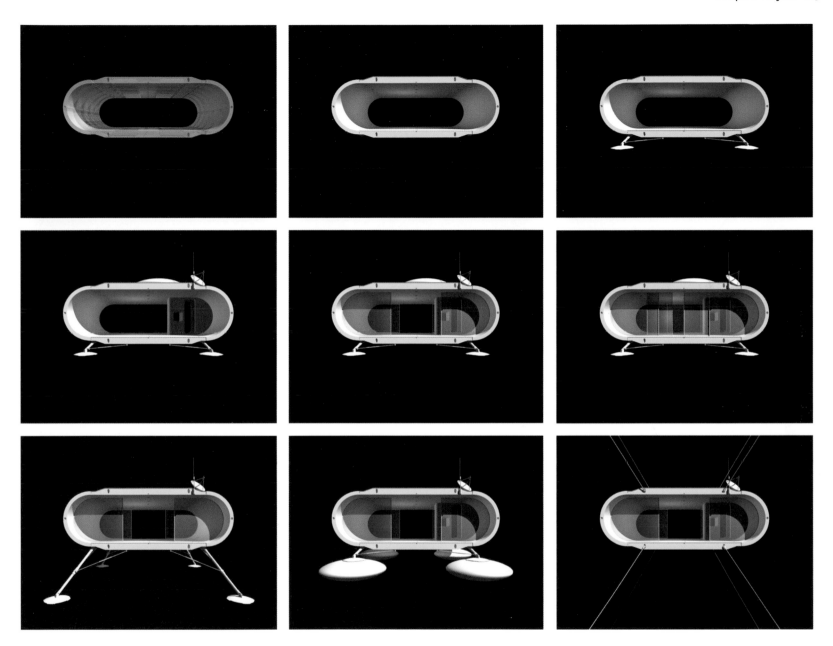

The Lifepod is a computer-generated model conceived as a multipurpose cabin.
As of yet, the first prototypes have not been built.

Sauna

Architect: Ari Bungers

Location: Pirunsaari Island, Finland

Photos: Ari Bungers

Structural system:

Metal rings and extendable tubes to support a wood-framed structure

Materials:

Steel and wood

Type of tree:

Pine

The goal of this project was to design a tree house that would primarily function as a typical Finnish sauna. The site is located on a small uninhabited island about 300 miles north of Helsinki, in the company of only two small houses that remain out of sight from where the tree house stands. The inaccessibility of the area, which can only be reached by taking a long walk after a short boat ride, has managed to preserve the rich and delicate vegetation of the island, mainly composed of tall pine trees, shrubs, and wild berries. Any trails that were ever created have been grown over by a thick layer of vegetation that blankets the terrain. In order to have the least possible impact on the landscape, the tree house was completely suspended above the ground, creating the sensation of a floating object within the forest. The project houses the basic living areas—including a dining area, terrace, sauna, and bedroom—leaving the service areas and other functions to the nearby houses that can be accessed by way of bridges that also hang from the trees.

The ground can be accessed from the suspended bridges or from the tree house itself.
The project is currently undergoing the technical phase of development and is planned
to function as a sauna in the summer of 2006.

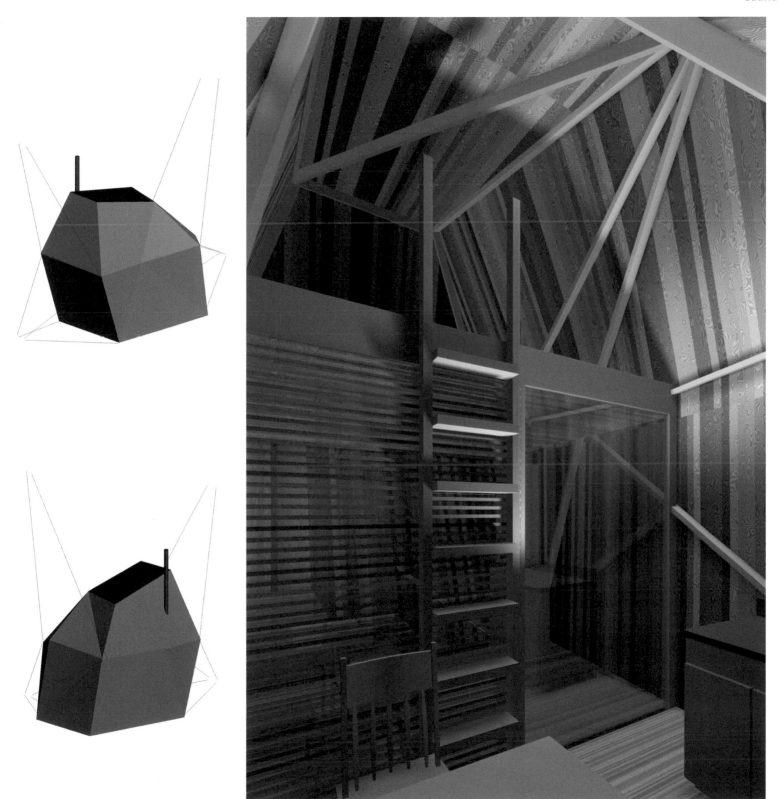

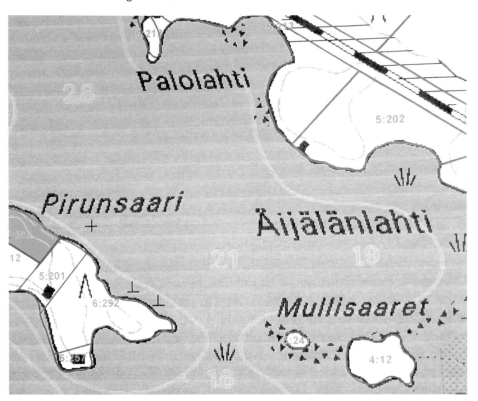
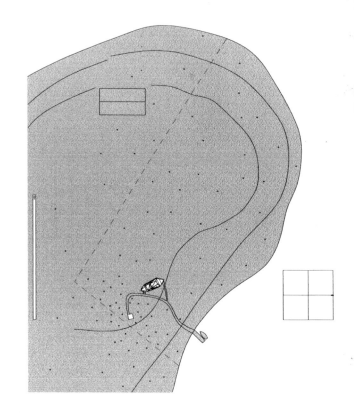

Location plans

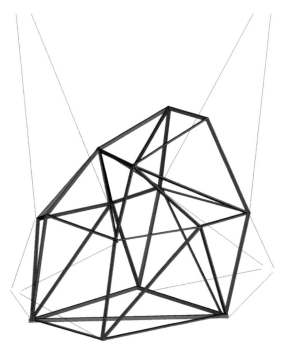
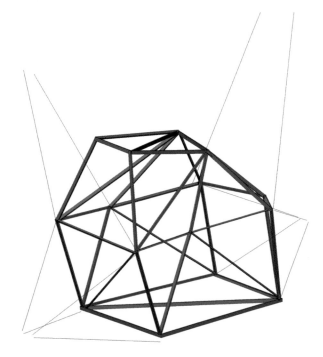

Structural diagrams

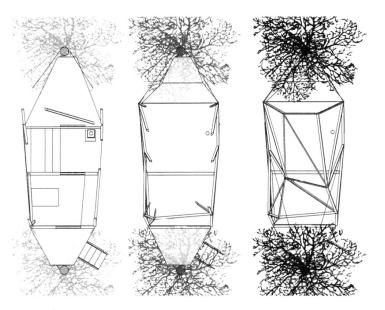

Floor plans

Section

Terrace Tree House

Architect: Alain Laurens
Location: Saint Rémy de Provence, France
Photos: Pere Planells

Structural system:

Wooden brackets supported by
the trunk and iron pillars for
the stairway

Materials:

Cedar wood and wrought iron

Type of tree:

Plane

Saint Rémy de Provence is located in the south of France and is known for its landscape, architecture, and cultural heritage. The outskirts are home to important examples of Roman architecture and art that have been preserved until now in the form of public buildings, hotels, and villas that accommodate large yards designed in the local style. Rather than a house inside a tree, this structure consists of a small viewing platform designed to integrate and interact with the historical area in which it is situated. The platform, located along the main branch of a sturdy plane tree, was conceived as a continuation of the series of out-door spaces that compose the yard. The structure of the tree house itself conforms to the spiral composition that envelops the trunk, beginning with a broad, curved stairwell and finishing with a viewing platform on the upper level. The structure of the staircase and the handrail that runs the length of the platform were made out of iron rods, generating a sense of transparency and lightness throughout. The landscape design was carried out by Dominique Lafourcade / Bureau d'Etudes Bruno & Alexander Lafourcade.

The detailed finishings, such as the handrail or the bas-relief of the stairs, give this small structure a refined appearance.

The access stairwell and platform are defined by a handrail made from black, slender, wrought-iron bars that generate a light, transparent appearance and integrate harmoniously and aesthetically with this historical area.

Luberon

Architect: Alain Laurens
Location: Provence, France
Photos: Pere Planells

Structural system:

Wooden rings around the
trunk and wooden brackets
supporting the platforms

Materials:

Cedar wood; plywood sheets
for the roof

Type of tree:

Mediterranean pine

As a rule of thumb, tree houses should be built in the lower part of the tree. This guarantees certain conditions that favor the durability of the tree house, given that it is more protected from wind, the swaying of the tree, and the growth of new branches. On the other hand, a tree house situated at a greater height can also provide advantages if an appropriate tree is chosen and carefully studied so that its physical characteristics are suitable for the new construction. The tree house's role as a place of refuge, fantasy, and observation becomes that much more evident when it is situated on a treetop. This is the case of this small tree house set atop a robust Mediterranean pine in the south of France. In order to access the tree house, a steep ladder was built and divided into two flights that lead directly to the closed area of the structure. The interior is equipped with electricity, a storage area, and a full set of furnishings to accommodate guests for long periods of time.

This staircase, divided into two flights of wooden steps, was constructed on the highest point of the slope in order to reduce the distance between the ground and the treetop.

The platform extends toward the exterior, generating a lookout deck
from which to enjoy the panoramic views of the area.

Fredericks

Architect: TreeHouse Company

Location: West Sussex, UK

Photos: TreeHouse Company

Structural system:

Wooden beams and pillars; rubber rings around the tree

Materials:

Red pine, cedar planks, wood branches, and stainless steel

Type of tree:

Scottish pine

This tree house is located right on the ege of a historical estate in West Sussex, UK, partly hidden inside a broad meadow defined by heavy-framed and medium-sized trees. An old, sturdy Scottish pine serves as the main support for this structure that combines red pine, used in the majority of the cabin; cedar, used to construct the roof; and noble tree branches, used for the balustrade. The tree house consists of a small room surrounded by a spacious balcony whose composition reflects the dual character of the project. A steep staircase on the side of the balcony integrates with the forest and leads to the platform which is situated about 9 feet above the ground and is adjacent to a slide—ideal for children at play. On the opposite side, the balcony takes on a rounded shape that allows for the passage of a large branch and creates a quieter, more contemplative area for adults.

The front part of the balcony that surrounds the cabin curves
to accommodate one of the main branches of the pine tree on which it rests.
Small wooden branches were used to define the handrail.

The use of only a few core materials creates a uniformity within the dwelling.

The flooring is wood parquet and the walls are plastered.

In the kitchen, stainless steel combines with the painted white wood of the cupboards.

General elevation

Leveled Tree House

Architect: Alain Laurens

Location: Aix-en-Provence, France

Photos: Pere Planells

Structural system:

Wooden cantilevers attached to the tree and wooden pillars in the ground for the bridge

Materials:

Oak and Pine

Type of tree:

Beech

The location of this small wooden house, situated on the border of a steep incline, served as the starting point for this project found in Aix-en-Provence in the south of France. The goal of the design was to preserve the characteristics of the topography, as well as the dense wooded forest that gave way to clear views of the distant horizon. The inclination of the terrain was utilized to situate the tree house in the central area of the tree and connect it to the home by means of a long footbridge situated at ground level. The structure consists of a series of slender brackets anchored into the tree to serve as supportive pillars. The bridge that connects the two houses rests on a central wooden support anchored into the ground. The same wood as that used inside the home was chosen for the tree house, emphasizing the connection between the two dwellings. The tree house is used as an extension of the home, a playground, or a guest room for temporary visits. The landscape design was carried out by Dominique Lafourcade / Bureau d'Etudes Bruno & Alexander Lafourcade.

The existing old house, situated at the foot of a small hill,
determined not only the height of the construction,
but also the typology chosen and materials employed.

The single access to this tree house through the house terrace provides extreme privacy.

Getty

Architect: TreeHouse Company
Location: Buckinghamshire, UK
Photos: TreeHouse Company

Structural system:

Wooden cantilevers and beams
attached to the tree

Materials:

Red cedar for the walls, floors,
windows, and doors; Canadian
cedar planks for the roof

Type of tree:

Cedar

The owner of this tree house wanted to take advantage of the large yard situated within her property in Buckinghamshire, in the heart of England. The idea was to create a quiet space away from the hectic pace of the home in which to read, meditate, and enjoy the privacy offered by the surrounding foliage. The project consists of a comfortable tree house constructed of cedar wood and situated in a cedar tree, with views of the nearby lake and landscape beyond. The client requested that the cabin have easy access and be useable throughout the year. In response to these requirements, a wide cedar staircase was built to access the tree house, while the interior was fitted out with heating and double-glazed windows for a comfortable atmosphere. Simple furnishings composed of layered rugs, cushions, chairs, and a bed serve to complement the warm and cozy environment that the client was seeking.

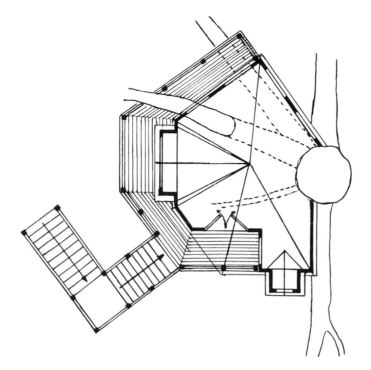

Floor plan

Elevation

Bisley

Architects: Tom Howard, James Foottit, Thomas Millar
Location: Bisley, Gloucestershire, UK
Photos: Melissa Moore, Thomas Millar

Structural system:

Wooden floorboards supported by the tree and supplementary wooden columns

Materials:

Oak and various types of recycled wood.

Type of tree:

Dead oak

This tree house is located in the yard belonging to the parents of the architect in charge of the project. Ever since the family moved to this house and began to work on the yard, they detected the presence of an old, robust oak tree that was dying. As the years passed, the tree gradually lost its remaining foliage and was reduced to a sinuous but solid skeleton that the owners did not wish to remove from the site. The architect proposed taking advantage of its presence by building a tree house that would serve as a small refuge in the middle of the yard. The cabin was to be made as accessible to the children as it would be to their grandmother, and was also to preserve an old swing that hung from one of its branches. The tree house would also serve as a place from which to contemplate the yard from a different perspective. The construction, which required a crane and the services of a professional gardener to remove the dead branches of the tree, took advantage of all of the wood to fabricate the structural frame, balcony, and roof planks.

The rectangular wooden sections used for the construction and finishings of this tree house, which vary in size and proportion, create a rich texture that changes depending on the angle from which the tree house is observed.

A broad, comfortable staircase leads to the refuge, whose lack of walls is mitigated by a large roof structure that provides protection and shelter from the climatic conditions if slept in overnight.

Floor plan

Elevations

Falcon

Architect: TreeHouse Company
Location: Fife, Scotland, UK
Photos: TreeHouse Company

Structural system:

Wood cantilevers supported by the tree trunk and complementary braces supported by the ground

Materials:

Cedar, cedar planks, Douglas fir, and copper sheets

Type of tree:

Cedar and copper beech

Located on the eastern coast of Scotland, approximately 30 minutes from Edinburgh, Fife is a region rich in architectural heritage and known for its grand coastal villas, the historical capital of Dunfermline, and its old forests and marine landscapes. The surroundings constitute an ideal site for this tree house, designed to create an imaginary world for children and adults alike inside the grounds of an old country home. The clients wished to make use of an existing cedar tree, which had been reduced to a pair of robust branches and scarce foliage after having been hit by lightning on two occasions. Situated adjacent to a beech tree, the project aimed to join both trees by a tree house that would serve as a playroom for the children. The construction consists of two platforms, joined by a bridge, one of which remains open to obtain splendid views of the yard, and another enclosed platform that takes on a circular form reminiscent of the old castles of the region.

The fairy-tale-like character of this construction is reflected
in even the smallest of details, such as the metal tops of the conical roofs,
the stylized window designs, and the curved wooden handrail.

A 500-year-old cedar tree and a beech tree harbor this small story-book construction.

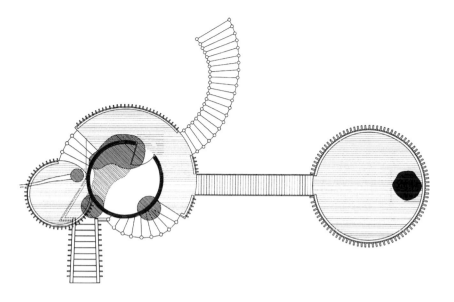

Floor plan

Elevation

Section

Omaha

Architect: Randy Brown Architects

Location: Omaha, NE, USA

Photos: Randy Brown

Structural system:

Platform partially supported by the trunk's branches and a portico of wooden pillars and beams

Materials:

Cedar wood for the structural elements and general finishings; corrugated metal sheet for the roof

Type of tree:

American oak

This project is the result of a summer course in which architects and students participated in developing the design and construction of this tree house. The main objective was to create a playground for the leading architect's two children that would also cater to adults for the purpose of experiencing the magical atmosphere that surrounds these structures. A specific focal point was chosen to capture the most stunning panoramic views of the landscape, while implementing elements that enclosed the space for the safety of the young ones. All of the exterior lookout points were marked off by screens that provide views as well as security. The tree house can be accessed by a staircase that incorporates the lower branches of the tree, by way of a ramp, or by ropes that hang directly from the main room. The project was designed and constructed by the Randy Brown summer workshop including: Steve Mielke, Matt Stoffel, Ted Slate, Katy Atherton, David Marble, Pavel Pepeliaev, Hill Corcovan, Scout Shell, Mathew Meehan, and Mathew Miltner.

The characteristic elements that make up the general composition of this project define each area, such as the access stairway composed of steps anchored into the trunk.

During the construction process, which lasted nine weeks,
many of the ideas conceived throughout the previous three weeks proved to be unfeasible
in light of the site's conditions and the reality of the construction.

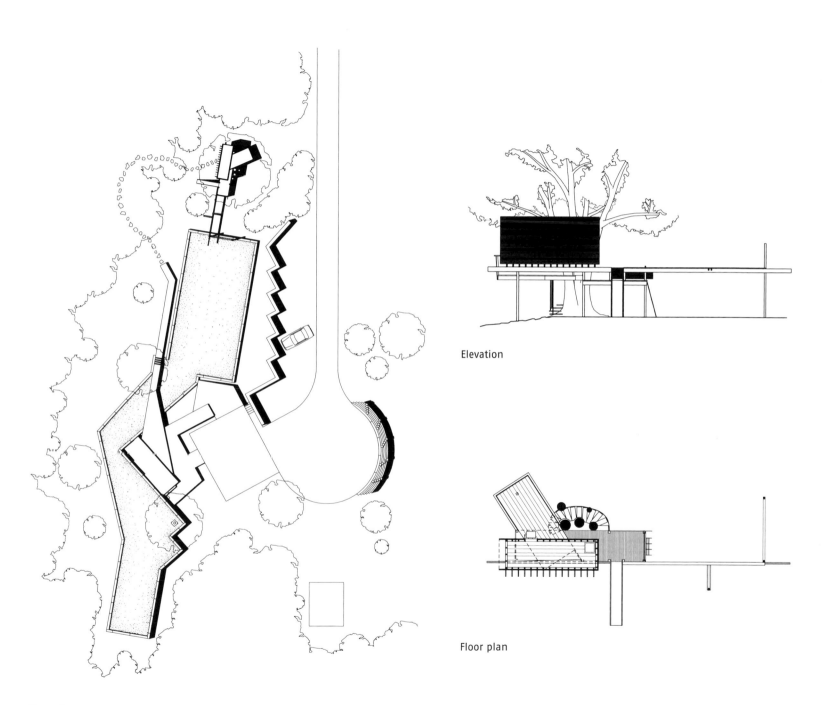

Floor plan

Elevation

Floor plan

Tree House

Architect: 24H Architecture
Location: Glaskogen, Sweden
Photos: Christian Richters

Structural system:

Wooden colums and beams

Materials:

Cedar

Type of tree:

Any type of tree

Rather than depending on a tree for support, this freestanding tree house blends into the landscape to become one with the surrounding forest. The structure consists of an extension to an old cabin on the shores of the Övre Gla Lake, located in Sweden's Glaskogen nature reserve. Local regulations placed a limit on the amount of surface area to be constructed and also required that the structure remain as far back from the shore as possible. These restrictions led the architects to create an object that would take up a minimum amount of space and adapt to the environment in terms of climate, season, or number of occupants. The project consists of a double skin that wraps the structure to protect it from low temperatures during wintertime. In summer, the exterior skin can be folded outward to create a series of outdoor terraces, uniting the house with the landscape to create a sense of openness that extends toward the lake.

In constructing the roof and exterior finishings, the architects employed traditional materials
and local construction techniques in new and innovative ways.
The cedar wood, with time, will gradually take on the tonalities of the surrounding landscape.

Composed of overlapping slender wooden sheets in the form of a traditional tile roof, the exterior cladding camouflages this tree house within the landscape and serves as the project's most characteristic feature.

Lee

Architect: Joseph Lim
Location: Gallop Park, Singapore
Photos: Ismurnee Khayon

Structural system:

Slender metal column structure supported by the ground, and wood for the balconies

Materials:

Steel and wood

Type of tree:

Tembesu from Singapore

The client for this project wanted a recreational space in the yard of his private home that could be used as a gathering place for children and adults. One of the trees located on the site—the tembesu, a large and vibrant species common to Singapore—served as the starting point for the project. This particular tree, a mature specimen dating back to the 19th century, is protected by the Singapore National Parks Committee. Despite its age, it is healthy and tall, and boasts a significant amount of foliage in relation to its slender, 3-foot-diameter trunk. Adjacent to the tembesu, a smaller tree—referred to as the jering—bears fruit with medicinal properties. Both possess extensive roots that radiate in all directions. The structure of this tree house, which is mainly sustained by the ground, had to be carefully positioned in order to create a series of habitable platforms without damaging the trees' complex root systems. The goal of the upper level's design was to generate a structure defined by the branches of the tree that would simultaneously permit movement and growth.

This project was carefully studied so that the structure would not interfere with the tree, yet would still maintain a close relationship with its shape. The wooden planks along the exterior siding, for example, are interrupted by small branches that pass through the structure.

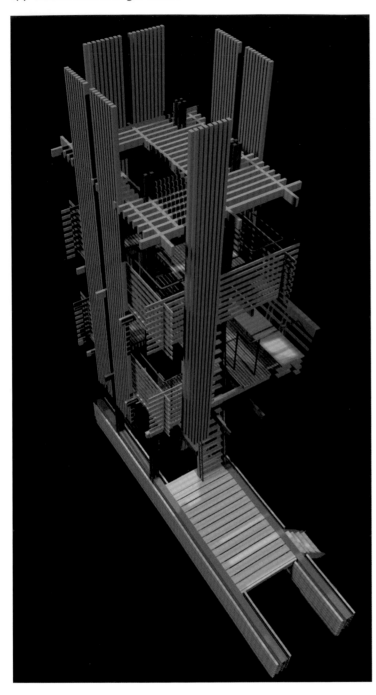

The tree house is composed of two upper balconies, which are integrated with the foliage and from which one can obtain panoramic views of the landscape.
A lower balcony is situated three steps from the ground and serves as a patio.

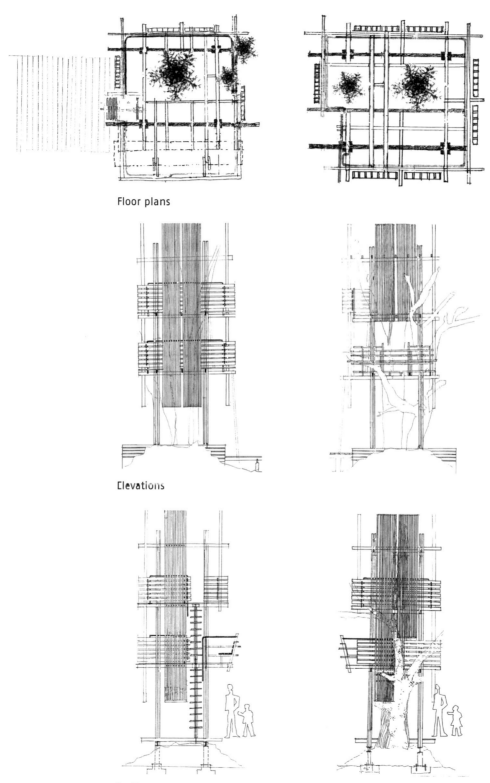

Floor plans

Elevations

Sections

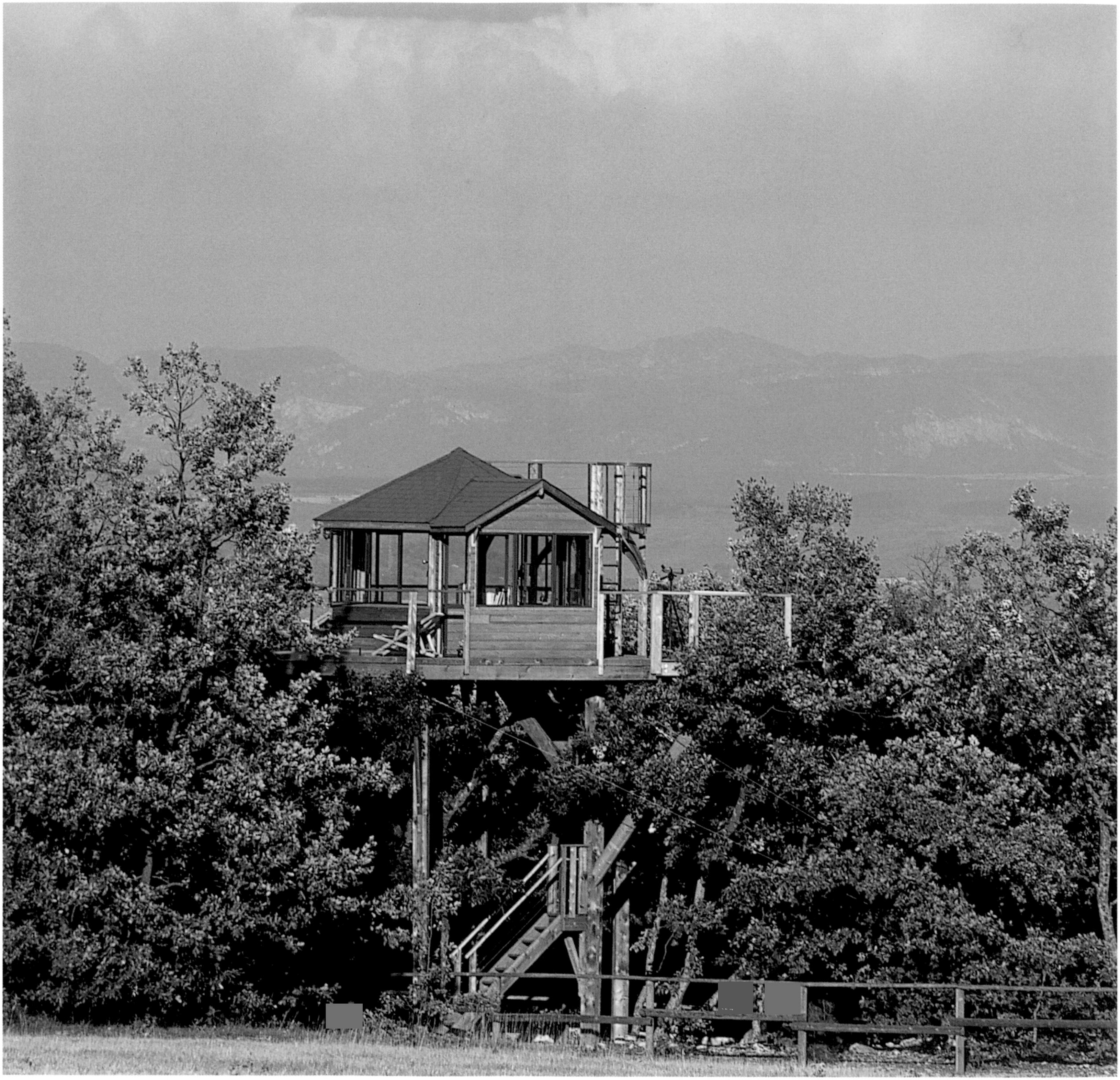

Observatory Tree House

Architect: Alain Laurens
Location: Provence, France
Photos: Pere Planells

Structural system:

Wood portico system supported by the ground

Materials:

Cedar and pine wood

Type of tree:

Any type of tree

Although this structure does not incorporate the tree trunks as partial or total support, its configuration, structure, and integration with the neighboring treetops make it worthy of being referred to as a tree house nevertheless. The clients of this property in Provence, in the south of France, wished to take advantage of the wonderful views obtained from their heavily wooded grounds. The tree house consists of a spacious room where the clients can relax or spend the night. The structure is composed of a radial system of wood columns that sustain the tree house approximately 20 feet from the ground. An exterior terrace that surrounds the room on three sides allows for panoramic views at any time of the day, while the glass enclosure emphasizes the integration between interior and exterior.

This tree house is accessed by a long wooden staircase
located on the upper side of the site.

Tree Canopy

Architect: 51%studios architecture, Alastair Townsend

Location: Virtual

Photos: 51%studios architecture, Alastair Townsend

Structural system:

Virtual

Materials:

Virtual

Type of tree:

Virtual

This project initially began as an exercise in imagining how to generate a tree with a computer. After analyzing the systems and programs that are capable of arranging these configurations through the use of fractals, the architects discovered the possibilities of creating a structure based on a flexible network and re-creating many of the characteristics pertaining to a tree, such as its form and structure. They also visualized the possibility of creating a habitable space of open, interconnected cells with enough space in which to sleep or from which to enjoy the views: a refuge suspended within a portable structure. This habitable tree would be firmly anchored to the ground by cables tightly fastened to deep layers of the terrain, which would permit the creation of a network of branches, bridges, and platforms on the upper area. The trunk is stabilized with bricks that can also be used to create a cooling cylinder for collected water. By climbing the tree, one can access platforms of diverse hardness and opacities that can accommodate spacious communal areas, as well as individual zones for sleeping or contemplating the landscape.

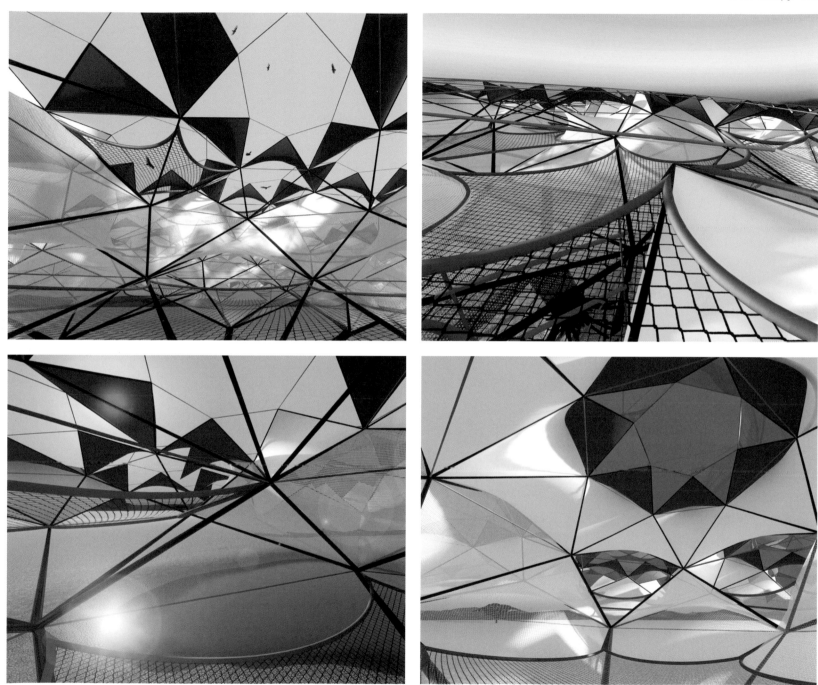

The complex system of metal supports, membranes, and webs creates an interior landscape that opens up to permit views of the sky and surrounding scenery.

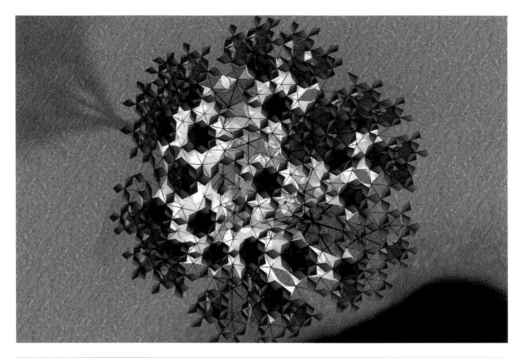

The web that composes this large roof structure permits the creation of a series of open, illuminated spaces. The lowest platforms also enjoy views of the sky.

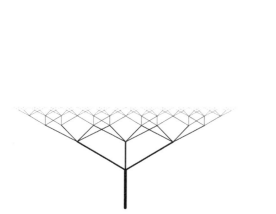

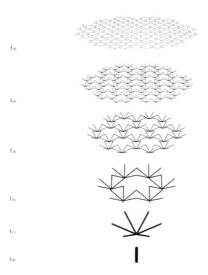

Fractal studies

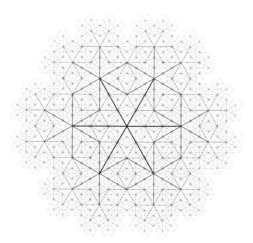

Plans

24H Architecture
Van Nelleweg 1206, Tabak 2.06, Rotterdam 3004 HE, Netherlands
T: +3110-7503150
F: +3110-7503160
info@24H-architecture.com
www.24H-architecture.com

51%studios architecture
The Ziggurat 60-66, Saffron Hill, London EC1N 5QX, UK
T: +44 207 632 4810
F: +44 207 632 4811
info@51pct.com
www.51percentstudios.net

Alain Laurens
La Cabane Perchée
La Campagne Bertet, Bonnieux 84480, France
T+F: +33 4 90 75 91 40
F+F: +33 1 47 90 46 73
info@ la-cabane-perchee.com
www.la-cabane-perchee.com

Andreas Wenning / baumraum
Roonstrasse 49, Bremen 28203, Germany
T: +49 421 70 51 22
a.wenning@baumraum.de
www.baumraum.de

Andrew Maynard Architect
2 Erskine Place, North Melbourne, Victoria 3051, Australia
T: + 61 0425 726 131
F: + 61 9329 3778
andrew@andrewmaynard.com.au
www.andrewmaynard.com.au

Ari Bungers
Pursimiehenkatu 14, Helsinki 00150, Finland
T: +358 9 622 4040
F: +358 9 622 4044
www.LAB–arkkitehdit.fi

Jeff Etelamaki
45 Main Street, Suite 903, Brooklyn, NY 11201, USA
T: +1 718 243 9088
F: +1 718 243 0454
jetelamaki@aol.com

Joseph Lim Ee Man
4 Architecture Drive, Singapore 117566, Singapore
T: +65 687 43 528
akilimem@nus.edu.sg
www.josephlimdesigns.com

Kyu Che Studio
38 Lusk Street 5, San Francisco, CA 94107, USA
T: +1 415 425 3191
F: +1 208 460 2299
kyu@kyuche.com

Mithun Architects
Pier 56, 1201 Alaskan Way, Suite 200, Seattle, WA 98101, USA
T: +1 206 623 3344
F: +1 206 623 7005
www.mithun.com

Randy Brown Architects
1925 North 120th Street, Omaha, NE 68154, USA
T: +1 402 551 7097
F: +1 402 551 2033
www.randybrownarchitects.com

Santiago Cirgueda
Recetas Urbanas
sc@recetasurbanas.net
www.recetasurbanas.net

Softroom
341 Oxford Street, London W1C 2JE, UK
T: +44 20 7408 0864
F: +44 20 7408 0865
imogen@softroom.com
www.softroom.com

Tom Howard, James Foottit, Thomas Millar
3 Wormwood Hill, Horsley, Gloucestershire GL6 0PP, UK
T: +44 7814 020 993
tomas@omnivorist.org
www.omnivorist.org/mhw

TreeHouse Company
The Stables, Maunsheugh Road, Fenwick, Scotland KA3 6AN, UK
T: +44 1560 600111
F: +44 1560 600110
info@treehouse-company.com
www.treehouse-company.com

Urban Studio
878 Peachtree Street, Atlanta, GA 30309, USA
T: +1 404 876 7499
F: +1 678 623 0847
ustudio@urbanstudio.us
www.urbanstudio.us